Somewhere Over The Rainbow

Veloisa Diana Simpson

With Misha McConnell-Todman

Published and Distributed by:
Professional Publishing House
1425 W. Manchester Ave., Suite B
Los Angeles, California 90047
www.professionalpublishinghouse.com
Drrosie@aol.com
(323) 750-3592

Cover design: TWA Solutions
First printing:
ISBN: 978-0-9891960-8-6
Library of Congress Control Number: 2013956211
10987654321

ACKNOWLEDGMENTS

A *special thanks* to all the people who played a significant role in my life:

1. Nancy Johnson (Mosquito)
2. Deni Pavon (Angel)
3. Catherine McCarns-Johnson (Precious)
4. Kim Jackson (Sunshine), my Godchild
5. Sharron Williams (Firecracker)
6. Misha McConnell-Todman (Turtle Dove)
7. Billie Barrett (Ringing Bell)

Thank you, Veloisa Diana Simpson (The Squirrel)

Through pain and sickness, I know and believe that the spirit of God within me gave me Time, Wisdom, Strength, and Energy to write and finish this book,

Somewhere Over The Rainbow

About the Author

*V*eloisa Diana Simpson was born in Indianapolis, Indiana. After completing Crispus Attucks High School, Veloisa entered West Virginia State University and graduated with a Bachelor of Science Degree in Education. The following ten years Veloisa taught students at Robert Gould Shaw Elementary School. She decided to move to California to start a new chapter in her life.

Veloisa is a member of Alpha Kappa Alpha (AKA) Sorority, Inc., and Life Member of Theta Mu Omega Chapter of Inglewood, California. She holds a Master of Science Degree in Education from California Lutheran University. After educational accomplishments, she became employed as a Special Education Teacher for the Compton Unified School District (CUSD). Veloisa retired in 1986 from the CUSD. She was honored with a Certificate of Meritorious Service for twenty-seven years of an outstanding contribution and service to CUSD students, staff, and community.

Special Achievements:

Veloisa received recognition for outstanding classroom technique in "Behavior Modification." Certificate of Participation in fields testing the Social Learning Curriculum from Research and Development Center Mental Retardation at Yeshiva University.

She was also awarded outstanding "Teacher of the Year" (Parents and Students Relationship).

The Marquis, "Who's Who Publications Board" certifies that Veloisa Diana Simpson is one of the subjects listed in Who's Who Biographical Record Child Development Professional, First Edition—inclusion in which is limited to those individuals who has demonstrated professional competence in their own fields of endeavor and who thereby contributed significantly to the betterment of contemporary society.

Veloisa has written several articles in magazines for Special Education Teachers. In 1991, Certificate of Appreciation was presented to her for Reading is Fundamental (RIF) for Outstanding and Dedicated Service to the boys and girls of Raymond Avenue Elementary School in Los Angeles, California. Professional Publishing House presented a book unveiling celebration for Veloisa Diana Simpson, author of *Living The Life You Taught Me: Unforgettable Memoirs*.

TABLE OF CONTENTS

The Rainbow 9

Letters to God 11

God's Kingdom 25

Sunrise - Sunset 27

The Journey to God's Kingdom 29

Dedication to Sunrise - Sunset 31

A Blessing For Loved Ones 33

Sandy Hook Massacre: December 14, 2012

    Twenty Beautiful Children 37

    Eight Brave Teachers 56

Bless the Children 69

Prayers 71

Praying For World Peace 73

The Lord Is My Shepherd 75

From the Author 79

Remember Me 95

The Rainbow

❧

Rainbow…an arch of colors that appears in the sky opposite the sun and caused by the sun, shining through rain, mist or spray.

The Rainbow; when the sun shines after a shower of rain, we often see an arch of beautiful colors in that part of the sky opposite the sun. If the rain has been heavy, the bow may spread across the sky, and the two ends seem to rest on the earth below.

The cause of this interesting natural phenomenon is the reflection and refraction of the sun's rays falling on drops of rain, which creates the colors of the rainbow. The colors of the rain are an expression, which means a brilliant display of colors. There are seven colors in the bow, which includes violet, indigo blue, green yellow, orange, and red. These colors blend into each other so that the observer rarely sees more than four or five clearly.

There is a good deal of variation in the space each color takes up. This depends clearly upon the size of the raindrops in which any particular rainbow is formed. The rainbow is formed by sunlight; as the sun sets every evening, you only need to look to the sky to witness a sunset's magnificent shade of colors and light. May every sunset remind you of the presence of God… always with you and the people you hold close to your heart.

Letters to God

Heavenly Father,

I know You care when I _hurt_ and that You _hear_ me when I cry. I know that even when I feel _lonely_ and _unappreciated,_ I can dry my tears, lift my head, and greet the World with a _smile_ saying, "I am loved by my God."

Thank you,

Veloisa Diana Simpson

Heavenly Father,

In all my success, help me never to forget that what I am is more important than what I do. Remind me again and again that faith stimulates success, hope sustains success, but only love sanctifies success. I cannot and dare not succeed without your love and power in my life.

Love,

Veloisa Diana Simpson

Heavenly Father,

Oh My Precious Father, I am so grateful to You for the gift of fresh beginnings. Each day dawns with new opportunities and unexpected surprises. I will pursue the dreams that You set before me, and though I may face tough times, I know that with You I can soar above them.

Thank you,

Veloisa Diana Simpson

Heavenly Father,

It is good to sing praises to You in the morning to consider Your guidance during the day, and to remember Your faithfulness at sunset. It is right to celebrate with You in my successes. You are worthy of continual praise.

Love,

Veloisa Diana Simpson

Heavenly Father,

Look down upon me today and help me to live as Your ambassador. Make me a conduit of Your wondrous love. Let me see the importance of my simple life, the need You have even for me to be a part of Your plan, O' Lord, You are so good.

Love your child,

Veloisa Diana Simpson

Heavenly Father,

I thank you that I am alive with eyes to see the brightness of a new day and with ears that can hear. There is someone who loves me and that someone I know is You. Thank you for a beautiful life.

Love,

Veloisa Diana Simpson

Heavenly Father,

I remember the Ten Commandments for the thankful, thinking...

...be thankful for:

1) *Prayers answered*

2) *Healings seen and unseen*

3) *New-found friends*

4) *Impossibilities turned into possibilities*

5) *Gifts given*

6) *Self potential, and*

7) *Eternal hope*

Thank you Father,

Veloisa Diana Simpson

Heavenly Father,

Thank you Father, for a wonderful year. Thank you for an exciting future filled with positive unknowns that You make every tomorrow a thrilling adventure. I am so glad to be planning them with You. Bless them and fill them with Your righteousness.

Love,

Veloisa Diana Simpson

Heavenly Father,

O'Father, as I prepare to step into a new year may Your light of grace heal any hurts I have. May Your light of peace dissolve any anxiety. May Your light of love surround me. May Your light of courage uphold me as I move bravely ahead. Thank you, God My God.

Love,

Veloisa Diana Simpson

Heavenly Father,

O' Father, thank you for children. Your special gift to my world. Thank you for their laughter, their innocence, and their unquestioning trust. Make straight their paths and lead them from injuries or sickness. May they be called blessed, righteous, and glorious.

Thank you,

Veloisa Diana Simpson

Heavenly Father,

More than anything in the world, I want to grace in Your learning, wisdom, righteous, and faith. I always used to say, "I've got to see it to believe it." But instead, I am beginning to affirm, I've got to believe it before I see it!" Wow Father!!! I really must be growing.

Smile,

Veloisa Diana Simpson

God's Kingdom

God's Kingdom—A resting place of beauty, warmth and comforts where there are no days and years.

Somewhere Over The Rainbow

God's Kingdom is where I will lie down in peace. No more tears or pain. My loving Father will take me to His special home and that will be something greater than I could ever imagine. Always day and never night. No flu or colds. No sadness or hatred. No worries or fears. No goodbyes or deaths.

Sunrise ~ Sunset

Sunrise…………..........…...........……..……………..……..Sunset

Mothers…………………………...........…..........…………Mothers

Fathers…………………….....….......….…………..….…Fathers

Grandmothers…….…..….........................…..Grandmothers

Grandfathers……………...........................Grandfathers

Brothers…………………......................…...Brothers

Sisters………………….......................…….Sisters

Uncles…………...................................…..Uncles

Aunts…………...................................….Aunts

Nieces….......................................……Nieces

Nephews…...........................…..Nephews

Cousins…………,………Cousins

Friends……………..…..Friends

27

The Journey to God's Kingdom

Who Knew The Way

Who Followed The Path

Who Made the Journey

?

Dedication to
Sunrise ~ Sunset

This book is proudly and affectionately dedicated to all whom will have the glorious experience of living in this wonderful world. As well to those who have sunset *Somewhere Over The Rainbow*.

It Hurts To Lose
A Special Person

When death takes your special person, it hurts. The hurt is
real. It will be real in the days that follow. It will be real in the
months ahead. When sleep refuses to
come and loneliness refuses to leave.

When death takes your special person, it hurts on special days
like birthdays, anniversaries, Christmas,
and Thanksgiving.

Don't sit back and wait for those special days to overtake and
overwhelm you. Plan something nice for someone else. Those
special days will be not only bearable, but enjoyable.

It hurts to lose anyone who has a special place
in your heart.

After the death of your special person, there is still life for you. Let the Lord Jesus Christ be the healer of your broken heart. Someday you will be able to SMILE and say, my broken heart is healed.

Smile!!!

Veloisa Diana Simpson

A Blessing For Loved Ones

"The Lord watch between you and me, when
we are absent ones from the other."
—Genesis 31:49

Even though I cannot be with you, even though I cannot see
you or even talk with you, I am as close to you as a thought. I
am as near to you as the love I feel for you in my heart. When
I think of you, I bless you. My love encircles you through the
ends of the earth that separate us.

I do not worry about you. I know that the Lord is watching
over you. He is your health, your strength, your source of
supply, your happiness, and your peace of mind.

Wherever you are, God is there. Wherever I am, God is there.
He is watching over us while we are absent ones from the other
and making us know that we are forever one in Spirit.

Sandy Hook Massacre
December 14, 2012

20 Beautiful Children

Girls

Boys

Victims

Festive six-year-old Girl Scout lived her life with a gust. She was wearing her holiday outfit, a pink dress and white boots when she was killed.

Victims

Spunky six-year-old, who "loved gymnastics," said a close friend. Her efforts to entertain those around her earned her the nickname, "Silly Caroline."

Victims

Girls

Caring little six-year-old, a darling redhead with a "constant smile" was so passionate about animals.

Victims

Sweet angelic girl celebrated her seventh birthday just three days before she died. Neighbors hung purple balloons (her favorite color) on their mailboxes and gates.

Victims

Protective six-year-old, whose favorite colors were pink and purple. She loved her stuffed lamb animal. Her family said, "She was a great big sister to her little brother."

Victims

Artistic six-year-old, who loved to dance, was the daughter of a jazz musician.

Victims

Girls

Country-styled six-year-old, who loved horses. She had asked Santa for new cowgirl boots and a cowgirl hat.

Victims

Sociable seven-year-old, who loved art projects, soccer and gymnastics. She also loved playing dress-up.

Victims

Amusing six-year-old girl who had an infectious laugh.

Victims

Adventurous six-year-old, who had a pony and took horseback riding lessons. She liked Harry Potter books and the color red.

Victims

Cheerful six-year-old girl who had a sunny disposition.

Victims

Girls

Environmentalist six-year-old little girl, who liked to garden.

Victims

Boys

Competitive seven-year-old Cub Scout, who loved to ride his bicycle and play baseball with his dad. He had recently completed in—and won—his first mini triathlon.

Victims

Boys

Active six-year-old boy, affectionately known as "J" to family and friends, was a first grader. He loved baseball, basketball, swimming, arm-wrestling and riding his bike.

Victims

Boys

Brave six-year-old boy was killed after running into the hallway to help when he heard the cries of his distressed classmates.

Victims

Boys

Vivacious six-year-old boy who was incredibly loving.
He loved skiing, baseball, wrestling, and football.

Victims

Boys

Energetic six-year-old boy who loved bouncing on his backyard trampoline with his big brothers.

Victims

Boys

Fashionable seven-year-old boy with a freckled nose,
who loved his ripped jeans.

Victims

Boys

Loving six-year-old boy, who had an astonishing love for his family. His sister survived the massacre.

Victims

Musically inclined six-year-old boy, who loved The Beatles.

Sandy Hook Massacre
December 14, 2012

8 Brave Teachers

Victims

Forty-seven-year-old beloved Principal who died trying to protect her students.

Victims

Fifty-two-year-old Special Education Teacher, whose body was found in a classroom on top of children she was protecting.

Victims

Forty-seven-year-old beloved Principal who died trying to protect her students.

Victims

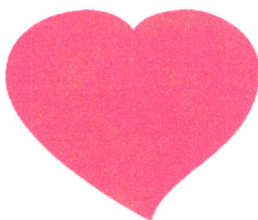

Fifty-two-year-old Special Education Teacher, whose
body was found in a classroom on top of children
she was protecting.

Victims

Twenty-seven-year-old, caring Teacher who saved the lives of many of her students by hiding them in a closet.

Victims

Thirty-year-old, passionate Teacher, whose life-long dream of being permanently hired by Sandy Hook was terminated upon her death.

Victims

Fifty-six-year-old School Psychologist who died while
confronting the gunman.

Victims

Twenty-nine-year-old Behavioral Therapist, who loved working with special needs children, lost her life.

Bless the Children

I bless the children with my thoughts and prayers. As children are going and returning from school, bless them and pray for them to have a positive enriching experience. I see them waiting for the school bus, anticipating a new school day; and I affirm it will be a good one. They are ready to learn about the world, other people, and themselves. Their minds and hearts are open. I envision each child discovering new skills, enhancing their natural talents, and putting new knowledge to use. Seeing the children excited about their day stirs a new enthusiasm in me. As a life-long learner and teacher, I look for and find a divine connection in the people and circumstances I encounter. My thoughts and prayers bless each child, as they are a blessing to the world.

Prayers

Now I lay me down to sleep
I pray to God my soul to keep
If I should die before I wake
I pray to God my soul to take

☙

Father, where I need strength today, I pray that I shall
receive it. Where I need healing, may it come and may
I accept it. Where I need courage and new enthusiasm,
may I open my heart and wait for it. Amen!

☙

Thank you, God, that I am alive, with eyes to see the
brightness of a new day, with ears that can hear the
singing of a bird, and with fingers that can feel the warmth
of your hand. There is someone who loves me, and I know
that someone is YOU. Thank you for a beautiful life. Amen!

☙

My Holy God, You have taught me to look for mountains and You give me courage to climb them. When I am bombarded by negative influences that try to pull me down, I do not despair for I remember Your promise, God, who has begun a good work in me, will complete it. Amen!

Jesus, it is because of You that I am able to look forward with anticipation, knowing You have prepared tomorrow for me and me for tomorrow. I come now, so thankful for the beautiful chapters of my life yet to be written, and for the happy endings that I cannot even imagine. Amen!

Thank you, Father, for making me brave when the road is rough; patient when the road is long; strong when the road climbs up; and most of all for giving me love when the road is lonely. When I felt alone in struggles, You were there to embrace me. Amen!

God, in praying, I bring the children of today to You. Bless their eyes with beautiful scenes of smiling faces and bless their ears with gentle sounds of loving people. And God, if they are exposed to horrific scenes, then grant them swift healing that life for them might be filled with Your joy. Amen!

Praying for World Peace

In the name of Jesus Christ, I pray for and decree a permanent peace, unity of all the nations of the world in a league of justice and righteousness, in which the life, liberty, and love of God shall be paramount. Prayerfully, I stand for peace. In my thoughts and prayers, I affirm peace for myself. I stand for peace no matter what the circumstance. I hold a vision of peace in the midst of conflict. I honor the dream of peace in each one of us.

My prayer and vision of peace in midst, when I serve as an understanding presence during a disagreement. Standing for peace, I encourage others to listen, to honor each other and to seek common ground. Every land, every nation includes people like me who are standing for peace. We are one in spirit, and our oneness generates true power. One by one, we stand for peace and together we bring it forth in our world.

O' God, protect our world upon who rest the responsibility for peace. Let wise counsel and unselfish arm prevail; bring peace to the countries that are filled with unrest and where righteous reformation is advancing, grant patience and fortitude to endure.

Peace begins when we recognize God in all creation, regardless of where or how we live. When we appreciate differences, celebrate our likeness, and acknowledge our oneness, we are taking initial steps toward world peace. People living in different nations vantage points; yet, we can still coexist in harmony. Respect and cooperation foster understanding, encouraging ingenuity boosts progress for all people. Everyone benefits when we find win-win solutions to social economic and ecological challenges. When we see rightly, we know we are one with each other and with God.

This is the beginning of World Peace...

The Lord Is My Shepherd

The Lord is my Shepherd. The Lord, God Almighty, maker of Heaven and Earth and all that exists! When I look through a telescope, peer into a microscope, or study nature, I get a glimpse of the amazing universe He created.

Thank you, Lord, for who You are and for all You have made.

The Lord of this universe calls me His precious child. He lovingly holds my life in His hands. Even though I can't see Him, He is here with me and will never leave me.

Lord, I'm amazed that You know me so well.

I am Blessed;
I have everything I need;
If you have God within your heart.

Lord, sometimes my worries and problems seem so big. But, they aren't too big for You, and I know You will take care of me in tough times.

He gives me strength.

Lord, I'm thankful that You're always ready to help me when I am in trouble. Thanks for your strength when I'm down.

Danger is everywhere.

Lord, sometimes I've been in danger and didn't even know it. Thank you for the times and many ways You've saved me from trouble.

Even if I walk through danger, I will not be afraid because You are with me.

Lord, You know everything that scares me. You even know the things I'm afraid might happen to me. I'm glad You're with me no matter what happens.

Lord, You have given me so much.

Thanks Lord, for all Your good gifts in my life, for a beautiful mother who showed me the three *L*s *(Look)* you will see... *(Listen)* you will hear... *(Love)* with your heart. You will live my special friends. Thanks for giving me all these joys because You love me.

Surely Your Goodness and Love will be with me all my life.
The Lord can be trusted in the seasons and storms of my life.
He has made very good plans for me and He holds
me close in His love.

Lord, I know that You will not leave me or quit loving me,
even when it seems that others do. I'm glad You don't ever
give up on me. Help me to confidently trust You
all the days of my life.

I will live in the house of the Lord forever…what a special
forever that will be. A new Heaven and a new Earth where
the sunsets rest in peace. No more tears or pain. My loving
Shepherd will take me to His special home, and that will be
something greater than I could ever imagine!

Lord, always day and never night. No flu or colds. No sadness
or hatred. No worries or fears. No more goodbyes or death.
I will see You face to face. I want to sit on Your lap and hug
You. You are my shepherd.

From the Author

When I wake up each morning, I will say to myself "I wonder what I will discover today." What I know for sure is that we learn something new every day.

Keep Smiling!!!
Veloisa Diana Simpson

Be open to new ideas...

Never stop learning and adapting. The world will always be changing forever. If you limit yourself to what you know and what you were comfortable with earlier in your life, you will grow increasingly frustrated with your surroundings as you age.

Have a purpose...

Without a purpose, nothing matters. You can work forty hours a week, come home to cook, clean, and then take up seventy-two new good habits, but if there isn't a reason you are doing it, none of these activities will mean anything to you.

Keep reading...

Those who read books benefit from what they learn and the entertainment they receive. In addition, they get to exercise their brain, and when that is done the feeling of satisfaction confirms how time is spent—wisely.

Trust...

May those you trust never betray you. May those you give your heart to always treat it well, with tenderness and respect. May the love you give to others come back to you tenfold.

Hold on to what matters the most...

In each loss, there is a gain, as in every gain there is a loss. As with each ending comes a new beginning.

Be socially supportive...

Take the time to help, comfort, or just be with those you care about when they are in need. You will feel good about your efforts and it will bring you an even closer relationship.

Tough times never last, but tough people do!!!

If you can dream it, you can do it!!!

Nothing is impossible!!!

Always be TRUE to yourself

Believe in the God who believes in you

Be happy you ARE loved

Rise above all challenges and live a life full of love, integrity and purpose

Success is never ending...failure is never final

Make each day your MASTERPIECE

Discover your possibilities...it's possible

Be careful...of your thoughts, for your thoughts become your words

Be careful...of your words, for your words become your actions

Be careful...of your actions, for your actions become your habits

Be careful...of your habits, for your habits become your character

Be careful...of your character, for your character becomes your destiny

Remember Me

Jesus, remember me when you enter
into your Kingdom of Heaven

Remember me with love

Love,

Veloisa Diana Simpson

(SMILE...)

www.ingramcontent.com/pod-product-compliance
Lightning Source LLC
Chambersburg PA
CBHW060744100426

42813CB00032B/3394/J